Alicia Ortego

I Can Enjoy Reading!

Visit us at **www.aliciaortego.com**

Paperback ISBN 978-1-959284-54-3
Hardcover ISBN 978-1-959284-47-5

This book
belongs to

I would give this book
(Rate this book)
Now I can

Come back to this page
after reading

This book is dedicated to those who read with delight,
To those who treasure books with all their might.
To those who enter worlds where magic streams,
And let their vivid imaginations shape their dreams.

To those who eagerly seek new things to learn,
To those unafraid, their wings unfurl and turn.
To those who share knowledge, facts, and fun,
This book's dedicated to you, each and every one.

Hey there, my name is Mia, turning eight this year.
Excited to tell you how books to me became so dear.

Reading first seemed quite dull, to be honest, I must say,
Until a new boy at school changed my mind one day.

Full of great game ideas, he was never a bore,
His smarts shone bright, his grades did soar.

With wisdom and mystery in all his replies,
He had us thinking he was an alien spy in disguise.

Sometimes he'd disappear,
out of sight,
His bag glowing softly,
in mysterious light.

We asked him, "What's inside?
Please do share!"
"Meet me by the chestnut tree,"
he said with a flare.

Waiting by the tree,
at the spot we all knew,
Wondering what was in the bag,
we had no clue.

"Full of farts, I bet!"
Lucas did shout,
"Watch them all fly
when he lets them out!"

"A hidden unicorn?" Sara guessed with a smile,
"Or an alien ship?" Leo mused for a while.

Yet, when the boy arrived, cheer in his measure,
He revealed, "Inside is my most precious treasure."

Eager to see, we gathered, excitement wide.
But at the sight of books, our spirits took a slide.

"Books?" we all gasped, a letdown hard to hide,
"Is there anything more dull you could've supplied?!"

"Books aren't dull, they're the best," he explained,
"You can be anyone, go anywhere," he maintained.

"To magical places where wonders lay,
Like in this book I started just yesterday."

We peeked in his book,
eyes open wide,
Superheroes inside,
on a fantastic ride.

Debating their powers,
who had the greatest fight,
Reading to find out
who had the most might.

Reading was joy, time just flew by,
Stopped only when the moon rose high in the sky.

"Where did this book come from?" we all did cry.
"I'll show you tomorrow," he said, with a twinkle in his eye.

My excitement soared,
sleep hardly came that night,
Dawn broke, and with it,
the secret came to light.

Calmly he led,
no fuss along the way,
"Ta-da!" he announced,
his treasure on display.

"A school library?"
In surprise, we all gazed,
Quickly seeing
where the magic blazed.
There were books galore,
for us all to feed,
So we started to search
for those we'd love to read.

"A book on football!"
Leo excitedly did shout.
"Is there one on unicorns?"
Sara asked, looking about.

Lucas cheered with delight,
"I found one about poop!"
And I chose the book about
my favourite music group.

What are your
favorite books?

Before we departed, the librarian did relay,
"Treat these books as treasures, gently, every day."

Around we huddled, like heroes taking a stand,
"We promise to care," we vowed, a pact so grand.

BOOK CARE RULES

Keep your library books away from food and drinks.

Always use a flat bookmark.

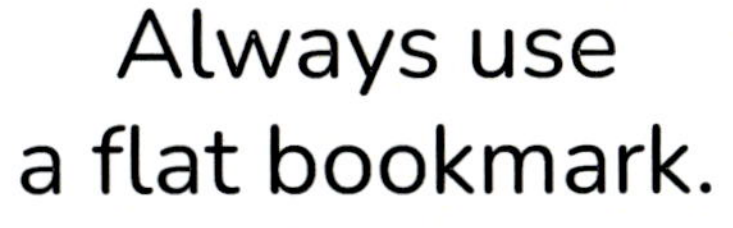

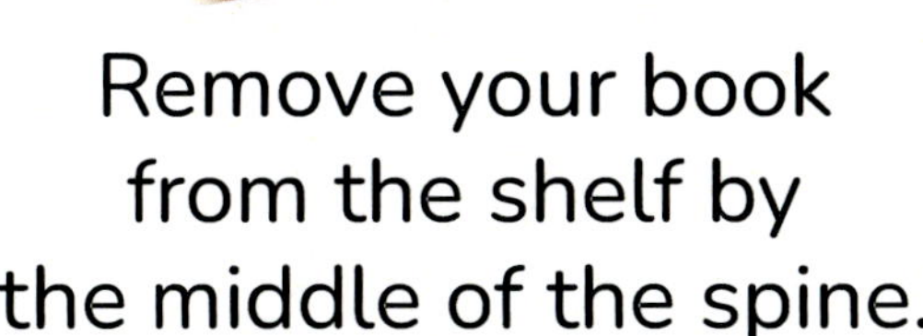

Remove your book from the shelf by the middle of the spine.

Do not draw, write, or color in or on a library book.

Be responsible and return your books on time.

Home at last, into my book I plunged with glee,
Marveling at amazing pictures my eyes ever did see.

I learned so much about the band I adore,
Their story inspired dreams of fame and more.

"Dino book!" my little brother came in with glee,
and made me read to him, snuggled close next to me.

I could not believe that before humans' birth,
for over 150 million years, dinosaurs ruled the earth!

The next day in class, my friends and I,
Shared our new knowledge, our spirits high.

"Unicorns don't have wings!" Sara said with surprise,
"Poop's mostly water!" Lucas claimed with pride.

We were eager to hear what more books had to say.
So, from the school library, we borrowed day by day.

I couldn't wait to discover new and exciting things.
I soon realised all the benefits that reading brings.

My posture's improved; no more eye strain,
Books over screens, the reason's plain.

I sleep better, my imagination in dreams never ends.
And there are more topics to talk about with friends.

Some kids couldn't see our bookish thrill,
Mocked our reading circle, with taunts to chill.

"Nerds! Geeks! Bookworms!" they jeered with all their might,
Yet we wouldn't let them dim our reading light.

Their words, just a charade, we brushed aside,
In our world of books, we'd joyfully abide.

Imagination's wings took us to new heights of play,
As our grades, like our spirits, rose day by day.

Reading's brought me so much joy, as you can tell,
Understanding grew, in its spell I fell.

School tasks became a breeze, so very light,
And my conversations shine, both day and night.

Reading's the magic that
binds us in friendship **tight**,
Sharing and learning,
in joy we **unite**.
Reading brings joy
and sets my spirit **free**,
Each page turned sparks joy,
enveloping **me**.

READING LOG

Date	Book Title	Pages/Minutes	Opinion

Dear reader,

Thank you so much for taking the time to read our book and share it with your little loved ones. We'd love to hear your thoughts. If you could spare two minutes to let us know how it made you feel, we would be very grateful. Your feedback is important to us and everyone else who is yet to read this book.

Alicia Ortego

BOOKS FOR KIDS

From the author

'I Can Enjoy Reading' is dedicated to every child who discovers the enchantment of books. As authors, our mission is to kindle a fervor for reading and nurture a fondness for storytelling in young hearts.

This book acts as a guiding light for parents, assisting them in introducing their children to the captivating world of literature. It's crafted to inspire children to embrace reading while equipping parents with valuable resources to support their journey.

Through Mia's adventures, young readers will uncover the wonders of imagination, the transformative power of knowledge, and the endless opportunities that books offer. We aspire for 'I Can Enjoy Reading' to ignite children's passion for literary exploration, encouraging them to embark on their own thrilling adventures in the realm of words.

'I Can Enjoy Reading' is one of the growth mindset books for kids created by Alicia Ortego. We believe that it's suitable for all ages and hope it will be enjoyed by all parents, grandparents, teachers and independent school readers.

Visit my website **www.aliciaortego.com** for more information and free printables or scan the code below.

Thank you again
for your support!
— Alicia Ortego

Other Books by Alicia Ortego

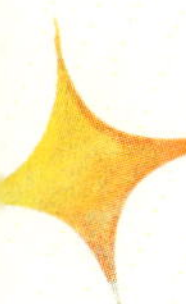

Made in United States
Orlando, FL
10 April 2025